Baby's Best
to knit and crochet

designs by Helen Passey

Leisure Arts Inc.
Maumelle, Arkansas

TABLE OF CONTENTS

GENERAL INSTRUCTIONS

ABBREVIATIONS

approx — approximately
beg — begin(ning)
BLO — back loop only
BO — bind off
ch(s) — chain(s)
CO — cast on
dc — double crochet(s)
dec — decrease(ing)
EOR — every other row
est — established
garter st — garter stitch (knit every row)
hdc — half double crochet(s)
inc — increase(ing)
K — knit
P — purl
patt — pattern
prev — previous
PSSO — pass slipped stitch over
rem — remain(ing)
rep — repeat
rib — ribbing
rnd(s) — round(s)
sc — single crochet(s)
sk — skip
sl — slip
sp(s) — space(s)
st(s) — stitch(es)
stock st — stockinette stitch (knit 1 row, purl 1 row)
TBL — thru back loop
tr — triple crochet(s)
tog — together
YO — yarn over

★ — work instructions following ★ as many **more** times as indicated in addition to the first time.
[ ] or ( ) — work enclosed instructions as many times as specified by the number immediately following **or** work all enclosed instructions in the stitch or space indicated.
† to † — work all instructions from first † to 2nd † as many times as specified by the number immediately following.
work even — work without increasing or decreasing in pattern established.

GAUGE

Correct gauge is essential for proper size of garments. Needle and hook sizes given in instructions are merely guides and should never be used without first making a swatch to check gauge.To test gauge, make a sample swatch approx 4" in the stitch, yarn and needle or hook specified. Then measure it, counting your stitches and rows carefully. If you have more stitches per inch that specified, try again with a larger size needle or hook. If fewer, try again with a smaller size. Keep trying until you find the size that will give you the specified gauge. DO NOT HESITATE TO CHANGE NEEDLE OR HOOK SIZE TO OBTAIN CORRECT GAUGE

CONVERSION CHART		
1 ounce	=	28.4 grams
1½ ounces	=	42.6 grams
2 ounces	=	56.8 grams
3½ ounces	=	99.4 grams
4 ounces	=	113.6 grams

POMPOM INSTRUCTIONS

Cut a strip of cardboard the width of desired size pompom. Wind yarn around cardboard, 80 to 100 times. Tie tightly in center and cut at opposite side. Trim ends evenly. To make 1" pompom, use a pencil instead of cardboard. Cut 8" length of yarn for tie and wind yarn 40 to 50 times around the pencil and 8" tie at the same time. Slide yarn off the pencil; tie tightly in center and cut at opposite side. Trim ends evenly.

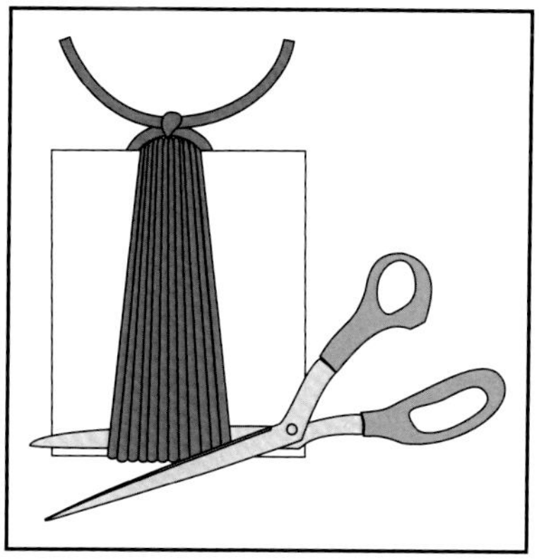

CROCHET TERMINOLOGY		
UNITED STATES		INTERNATIONAL
slip stitch (slip st)	=	single crochet (sc)
single crochet (sc)	=	double crochet (dc)
half double crochet (hdc)	=	half treble crochet (htr)
double crochet (dc)	=	treble crochet (tr)
treble crochet (tr)	=	double treble crochet (dtr)
double treble crochet (dtr)	=	triple treble crochet (ttr)
triple treble crochet (tr tr)	=	quadruple treble crochet (qtr)
skip	=	miss

KNIT TERMINOLOGY		
UNITED STATES		INTERNATIONAL
gauge	=	tension
bind off	=	cast off
yarn over (YO)	=	yarn forward (yfwd) **or** yarn around needle (yrn)

Knitted CARDIGAN

SIZES:	6 mos	12 mos	24 mos
Approx weight:	to 18 lbs	to 24 lbs	to 30 lbs
Body Chest:	19"	20"	21"
Garment Measurements:			
chest	20"	21"	22"
length to underarm	5 1/2"	6 1/2"	7 1/2"
sleeve length	6 1/2"	7 1/2"	8"

Size Note: Instructions are written in smallest size with changes for larger sizes in parentheses.

MATERIALS: Baby wt yarn, 4 oz (113.6 grams) peach; straight knitting needles size 3 (3.25 mm) or size needed for gauge; 5 (1/2") buttons; tapestry or yarn needle; 2 stitch holders.

GAUGE: In patt, 7 sts = 1"; 10 rows = 1"

Pattern Stitch

(***Note:*** Odd-numbered rows are right side rows; even-numbered rows are wrong side rows.)

Row 1: ★ K2, P2; rep from ★ across
Row 2: Rep Row 1.
Row 3: Knit across.
Row 4: Purl across.
Row 5: Rep Row 1.
Row 6: Rep Row 1.
Row 7: Purl across.
Row 8: Knit across.

INSTRUCTIONS

Back: CO 68(72-76) sts. (***Note:*** Mark Row 1 for right side.) Work Patt Rows 1-8. Rep Patt Rows 1-8 until piece measures $5^1/_2(6^1/_2-7^1/_2)$" from beg or desired length to underarm.

Armhole Shaping:

Rows 1 and 2: BO 4 sts at beg of row, work in est patt across: 60(64-68) sts.

Row 3: Continuing to work in est patt, dec one st each side EOR 3 times: 54(58-62) sts. Work in est patt until piece measures approx $3^1/_4(3^1/_2-4)$" from BO sts.

Shoulder Shaping:

Rows 1-4: BO 5(6-6) sts at beg of row, work in est patt across.

Rows 5 and 6: BO 5(5-6) sts at beg of row, work in est patt across. BO rem 24(24-26) sts.

Right Front: CO 37(41-45) sts. (***Note:*** Instructions are written for buttonholes on both sides. You can then sew buttons over unused buttonholes, sewing buttonholes closed as you sew on buttons. The placement of buttons then determines whether your sweater will be for a girl or for a boy.)

Row 1: (***Note:*** Mark for right side.) K5, place marker on needle, work Patt Row 1 on next 32(36-40) sts.

Row 2: Work Patt Row 2 across to last 5 sts, slip marker, K5. Keeping 5 sts in garter st (knit every row) at front edge, continue in est patt until 4 rows have been worked.

Row 5: Buttonhole Row: K1, K2 tog, YO, K2, work in est patt across. (***Note:*** If you adjust length, you must adjust spacing between buttonholes.) Continuing in est patt, rep Buttonhole Row every $1^3/_4(2-2^1/_4)$", 3 times more AND AT THE SAME TIME when piece measures same as back to underarm, ending by working right side row, work armhole shaping.

Armhole Shaping:

Row 1: BO 4 sts at beg of row, work in est patt across.

Row 2: Work in est patt across. Continuing in est patt, dec one st at armhole edge EOR 3 times: 30(34-38) sts. Work in est patt until piece measures approx 2" from BO sts ending at neck edge.

SIZE 6 mos ONLY: Neck Shaping: Row 1: K5, place sts just worked on holder for band, BO next 2 sts, continue in est patt across.

Row 2: Work even in est patt across. Continuing to work in est patt, BO 2 sts at neck edge EOR twice then dec one st EOR 4 times **AND AT THE SAME TIME** when armhole measures $3^1/_4$" from first armhole BO row, BO 5 sts EOR at armhole edge 3 times for shoulder shaping.

SIZE 12 mos ONLY: Neck Shaping: Row 1: K5, place sts just worked on holder for band, BO next 3 sts, continue in est patt across.

Row 2: Work even in est patt across.

Row 3: BO 3 sts at neck edge, continue in est patt across.

Row 4: Rep Row 2. Continuing to work in est patt, BO 2 sts at neck edge EOR 3 times AND AT THE SAME TIME when armhole measures $3^1/_2$" from first armhole BO row, BO 6 sts EOR twice at armhole edge, then BO rem 5 sts for shoulder shaping.

SIZE 24 mos ONLY: Row 1: K5, place sts just worked on holder for band, BO next 3 sts, continue in est patt across.

Row 2: Work even in est patt across. Continuing to work in est patt, BO 3 sts at neck edge EOR twice, BO 2 sts EOR twice, then dec one st EOR twice AND AT THE SAME TIME when armhole measures 4" from first armhole BO row, BO 6 sts EOR at armhole edge 3 times for shoulder shaping.

Left Front: CO 37(41-45) sts.

Row 1: (***Note:*** Mark for right side.) Work Patt Row 1 on first 32(36-40) sts, place marker on needle, K5.

Row 2: K5, slip marker, work Patt Row 2 across. Continuing in est patt, work same as Right Front reversing all shaping and working buttonholes to correspond with buttonholes on Right Front.

Sleeve: (make 2)**:**
CO 32(40-44) sts. (***Note:*** Mark Row 1 for right side.) Work Patt Rows 1-8. Working in est patt, when sleeve measures 1" from beg, inc one st each side. Continuing in est patt and working inc sts in patt, inc one st each side every inch 5 times more: 44(52-56) sts. Work even until piece measures $6^1/_2(7^1/_2-8)$" from beg.

Armhole: BO 4 sts at beg of next 2 rows, then dec one st each side EOR 15(14-16) times, then BO 0(4-2) sts at beg of each of next 0(2-4) rows. BO rem 6(8-8) sts.

Pocket (make 2)**:**
CO 18(20-22) sts.

Rows 1-3: Knit each row.

Row 4: K3, P 12(14-16), K3.

Row 5: Knit across.

Rep Rows 4 and 5 until piece measures approx $1^3/_4(1^3/_4-2)$" from beg. Work next 4 rows in garter st (knit every row). BO all sts; mark for bottom of pocket.

Finishing: With marked sides tog, sew shoulder seams, side seams and sleeve seams. Sew sleeves into armholes.

Neck Band: With piece right side facing, knit 5 sts from holder on right front, pick up and knit 15(19-20) sts from right front neck edge, 24(24-26) sts from back neck edge, 15(19-20) sts from left front neck edge, knit 5 sts from holder: 64(72-76) sts.

Row 1 (Dec Row)**:** K5(7-7), ★ K2 tog, K7(8-6); rep from ★ across to last 5 sts, K5: 58(66-68) sts.

Rows 2 and 3: Knit across.

Row 4: Buttonhole Row: K1, K2 tog, YO, knit across to last 4 sts, K2 tog. YO, K2.

Next 3 Rows: Knit each row. BO all sts. Sew one pocket on each front; sew on buttons; weave in any yarn ends.

Knitted DRESS

SIZES:	6 mos	12 mos	24 mos
Approx weight:	to 18 lbs	to 24 lbs	to 30 lbs
Body Chest:	19"	20"	21"
Garment Measurements:			
chest	20"	21"	22"
skirt length	$7^1/_2$"	$8^1/_2$"	$9^1/_2$"

Size Note: Instructions are written in smallest size with changes for larger sizes in parentheses.

MATERIALS: Baby wt yarn, 4 oz (113.6 grams) yellow; straight knitting needles sizes 2 (2.75 mm) and 3 (3.25 mm) or sizes needed for gauge; 2 stitch holders; $^1/_2$ yd ($^1/_8$") yellow satin ribbon.

GAUGE: With larger size needles in stock st,
6 sts = 1"; 9 rows = 1"

Special Note: Abbreviation TBL used in this pattern means "thru back loop".

Pattern Stitch

Row 1: ★ K5, YO ***(Fig. A),*** K2 tog, K1; rep from ★ to last st, K1.
Rows 2, 4 and 6: Purl across.
Row 3: ★ K3, K2 tog TBL, YO, K1, YO, K2 tog; rep from ★ to last st, K1.
Row 5: K1, ★ K1, K2 tog TBL, YO, K3, YO, K2 tog; rep from ★ across.
Row 7: ★ YO, work double dec as follows: K2 tog TBL, slip st just worked back onto left needle and pass next st on left needle over it ***(Fig. B)***; slip st just worked back on right needle (double dec made), YO, K5; rep from ★ to last st, K1.

Fig. A

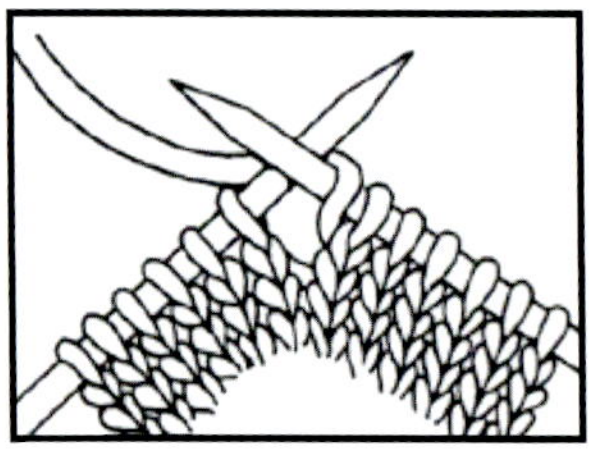

Fig. B

INSTRUCTIONS

Back: With larger size needles, CO 81(89-89) sts loosely. Work 4 rows in garter st (knit every row), then 4 rows in stock st (knit 1 row, purl 1 row). Work Pattern Stitch Rows 1-7. When pattern is completed, work in stock st until piece measures approx 6 1/2(7 1/2-8 1/2)" from beg or 1" less than desired length to underarm, ending by working a purl row.

SIZES 6 and 24 mos ONLY: Dec Row: ★ K2, K2 tog; rep from ★ to last st, K1: 61(67) sts.

SIZE 12 mos ONLY: Dec Row: (K2, K2 tog) 5 times, (K1, K2 tog) 15 times, (K2, K2 tog) 6 times: 63 sts.

ALL SIZES: Change to smaller size needles.

Rib Row 1 (wrong side)**:** P1, work in K1, P1 rib across.

Rib Row 2 (right side)**:** Work in K1, P1 rib to last st, end K1. Continue in est rib for approx 1", ending by working Rib Row 2. Change to larger size needles. Beginning with a purl row, work next 3 rows in stock st.

Armhole Shaping: Continuing in stock st, BO 2(2-3) sts at beg of next 2 rows, then dec one st each side EOR twice: 53(55-57) sts. Work even in stock st until piece measures approx 3 1/4(3 1/2-4)" from first armhole BO sts.

Shoulder Shaping: BO 5(5-6) sts at beg of next 2 rows, then BO 5 sts at beg of next 4 rows. BO rem 23(25-25) sts loosely.

Front: Work same as Back to top of ribbing. Change to larger size needles.

Placket: Row 1: P 28(29-31), K5, P 28(29-31).

Row 2: Knit across.

Row 3: Rep Placket Row 1.

Shaping armholes same as Back, continue in est patt until garter st placket measures approx 1(1 1/4-1 1/2)", ending by working a wrong side row.

Neck Opening: K 26(27-28), join 2nd ball of yarn and BO next st, knit across: 26(27-28) sts each side. WORKING BOTH SIDES AT ONCE, continue in est patt until placket measures approx 1 1/2(1 3/4-2)", ending by working a wrong side row.

Patt Row 1: K2(3-4), (YO, K2 tog, K6) 3 times; K7, (YO, K2 tog, K6) twice, YO, K2 tog, K1(2-3).

Patt Rows 2, 4 and 6: P 24(25-26), K4, P 24(25-26).

Patt Row 3: K0(1-2), (K2 tog TBL, YO, K1, YO, K2 tog, K3) 3 times, K2; K2, (K3, K2 tog TBL, YO, K1, YO, K2 tog) 3 times, K0(1-2).

SIZE 6 mos ONLY: Patt Row 5: K4, (YO, K2 tog, K1, K2 tog TBL, YO, K3) twice, YO, K2 tog, K4; K4, K2 tog TBL, YO, (K3, YO, K2 tog, K1, K2 tog TBL, YO) twice, K4.

Patt Row 7: (K5, YO, refer to instructions for Pattern Stitch and work double dec, YO) 3 times, K2; K2 (YO, work double dec, YO, K5) 3 times.

SIZE 12 mos ONLY: Patt Row 5: K2 tog TBL, YO, (K3, YO, K2 tog, K1, K2 tog TBL, YO) twice, K3, YO, K2 tog, K4; K4, K2 tog TBL, YO, (K3, YO, K2 tog, K1, K2 tog TBL, YO) twice, K3, YO, K2 tog.

Patt Row 7: K1, (K5, YO, refer to instructions for Pattern Stitch and work double dec, YO) 3 times, K2; K2, (YO, work double dec, YO, K5) 3 times, K1.

SIZE 24 mos ONLY: Patt Row 5: K1, K2 tog TBL, YO, (K3, YO, K2 tog, K1, K2 tog TBL, YO) twice, K3, YO, K2 tog, K4; K4, K2 tog TBL, YO, (K3, YO, K2 tog, K1, K2 tog TBL, YO) twice, K3, YO, K2 tog, K1.

Patt Row 7: K2 tog TBL, YO, (K5, YO, refer to instructions for Pattern Stitch and work double dec, YO) 3 times, K2; K2, (YO, work double dec, YO, K5) 3 times, YO, K2 tog.

ALL SIZES: Beginning with a purl row and keeping center sts in garter st, work in stock st until 1/2" above last row of patt.

Neck Shaping: Row 1: K 20(21-22), place next 6 sts on holder for left front, knit across.

Row 2: P 20(21-22), place next 6 sts on holder for right front, purl across. Continuing to work both sides at once, dec one st each side of neck every row, 5(6-6) times AND AT THE SAME TIME, when armhole measures same as Back, shape shoulder same as Back.

Sleeve (make 2)

With larger size needles, CO 26(32-38) sts loosely. Work in K1, P1 rib for 1". At end of last row, inc 1(1-0) st(s): 27(33-38) sts.

Next Row: K1(1-0), ★ inc in next st, K1; rep from ★ across: 40(49-57) sts. Work next 1(3-3) rows in stock st. Work Pattern Stitch Rows 1-7.

Sleeve Cap Shaping: Continuing in stock st, BO 2(2-3) sts at beg of next 2 rows, then dec one st each side EOR twice and every 4th row 2(3-4) times more: 28(35-39) sts.

Work 2 rows even. BO 2 sts at beg of next row.

Next Row: BO 2 sts, (K3 tog) 7(10-11) times, K2(0-1): 10(11-13) sts. BO rem sts.

Finishing: Sew shoulder seams, side seams, sleeve seams and sew in sleeves.

Neck Band: With smaller size needles, knit across sts from holder for right front, pick up 8(9-9) sts along right front neck edge, pick up 23(25-25) sts along back neck edge, pick up 8(9-9) sts along left front neck edge, knit across sts from holder for left front: 51(55-55) sts.

Next 3 Rows: Knit across.

Next 2 Rows: Decreasing one st each end of row, knit across.

Next Row: Knit across. BO all sts loosely. Cut 2, 9" lengths of ribbon. Sew 1 ribbon each side of front opening approx 1" above center BO st. Tie in bow.

Crocheted
RAINBOW SET

BLANKET, JACKET & BOOTIES

SIZE: Blanket: Approx 28" x 28"
Garments: Birth to 3 mos (to 13 lbs)

Garment Measurements:

chest	16"
length to underarm	5"
sleeve length	4"

MATERIALS: Baby wt yarn, 5 oz (142 grams) white, 1 oz (28.4 grams) each pink, apricot, lt yellow, lt green, lt aqua and lt lavender; aluminum crochet hooks size F (4.00 mm) **for Blanket and Booties only**, size D (3.25 mm) **for Blanket Squares only**, size E (3.50 mm) **for Jacket only**, or sizes needed for gauge; 2 yds (¼") white satin ribbon.

GAUGE: With D hook, 1 square = $1^{1}/_{2}$" x $1^{1}/_{2}$"
With E hook in patt, 8 sts = 1"; 3 rows =1"
With F hook in dc, 10 sts = 2"; 6 rows = 2"

INSTRUCTIONS

Note: Do not turn at end of rnds; blanket is worked on right side.

Blanket

With largest size hook and pink, ch 4; join with slip st in beg ch to form a ring.

Rnd 1: Ch 3, 2 dc in ring, ch 2, (3 dc in ring, ch 2) 3 times; join with slip st in 3rd ch of beg ch-3; finish off. Join apricot with slip st in any ch-2 sp.

Rnd 2: Ch 3, (2 dc, ch 2, 3 dc) in same ch-2 sp, ch 1, ★ (3 dc, ch 2, 3 dc) in next ch-2 sp, ch 1; rep from ★ around; join with slip st in 3rd ch of beg ch-3; finish off.

Rnd 3: Join lt yellow with slip st in any ch-2 sp, work beg corner as follows: ch 3, (2 dc, ch 2, 3 dc) in same ch-2 sp, ch 1 (beg corner made), ★ 3 dc in next ch-1 sp, ch 1; rep from ★ to next ch-2 sp, work corner as follows: (3 dc, ch 2, 3 dc) in ch-2 sp (corner made), ch 1; continue in same manner around entire square; join with slip st in 3rd ch of beg ch-3; finish off.

Rnd 4: With lt green, rep Rnd 3.

Rnd 5: With lt aqua, rep Rnd 3.

Rnd 6: With lt lavender, rep Rnd 3.

Rnd 7: With white, rep Rnd 3; at end of rnd, do not finish off, ch 4.

Rnd 8: Work in same manner as Rnd 3, having (3 dc, ch 1) in each ch-1 sp and (3 dc, ch 2, 3 dc) in each ch-2 sp to last ch-1 sp, 2 dc in ch-1 sp; join with slip st in 3rd ch of ch-4; finish off.

Rnd 9: Join white with slip st in any ch-2 corner sp, ch 1, 2 sc in same sp, hdc in next st, dc in each of next 3 sts, † ★ (2 tr, ch 2, 2 tr) in next st, dc in each of next 4 sts, skip next 2 sts, dc in each of next 4 sts; rep from ★ once, (2 tr, ch 2, 2 tr) in next st, dc in each of next 3 sts, hdc in next st, 2 sc in ch-2 sp, hdc in next st, dc in each of next 3 sts †; rep from † to † twice, [(2 tr, ch 2, 2 tr) in next st, dc in each of next 4 sts, skip next 2 sts, dc in each of next 4 sts] twice, (2 tr, ch 2, 2 tr) in next st, dc in each of next 3 sts, hdc in next st; join with slip st in beg sc; ch 3 (counts as dc).

Rnd 10: Dc in each st to next ch-2 sp, ★ (2 dc, ch 2, 2 dc) in ch-2 sp, [dc in each of next 4 sts, skip next 4 sts, dc in each of next 4 sts, (2 dc, ch 2, 2 dc) in next ch-2 sp] twice, dc in each st across to next ch-2 sp; rep from ★ 3 times, ending last rep dc in each of rem sts; join with slip st in 3rd ch of ch-3; ch 3: 18 dc each straight side.

Rnd 11: Rep Rnd 10; at end of rnd, join with slip st as before. Change colors as follows: drop white, draw pink thru loop on hook; with pink, ch 3: 22 dc each straight side.

Rnd 12: With pink, rep Rnd 10; at end of rnd change color to apricot: 26 dc each straight side.

Rnds 13-18: Rep Rnd 10, 6 times, continuing to increase 4 dc each straight side each rnd, and working 1 rnd in each of the following colors: apricot, lt yellow, lt green, lt aqua, lt lavender and white; at end of last rnd, finish off: 50 dc each straight side.

Rnd 19: With piece right side facing, join white with slip st in ch-2 sp of first ripple in any 3-ripple group, ch 1, ★ (sc in next dc, hdc in next dc, dc in next dc, tr in next dc, skip next 4 dc, tr in next dc, dc in next dc, hdc in next dc, sc in next dc, ch 1, skip next ch-2 sp) twice, sc in next dc, hdc in each of next 2 dc, dc in each of next 2 dc, [(2 tr, ch 2, 2 tr) in next dc, dc in each of next 3 dc, hdc in each of next 6 dc, dc in each of next 3 dc] 3 times, (2 tr, ch 2, 2 tr) in next dc, dc in each of next 2 dc, hdc in each of next 2 dc, sc in next dc, ch 1, skip next ch-2 sp; rep from ★ 3 times; join with slip st in beg sc; ch 3.

Rnd 20: Dc in each of next 24 sts (each ch-1 and each st), ★ [(2 dc, ch 2, 2 dc) in next ch-2 sp, dc in each of next 6 sts, skip next 4 sts, dc in each of next 6 sts] 3 times, (2 dc, ch 2, 2 dc) in next ch-2 sp, dc in each of next 33 sts (each ch-1 and each st); rep from ★ 3 times, ending last rep dc in rem 8 sts; join with slip st in 3rd ch of ch-3; ch 3: 37 dc each straight side.

Rnd 21: ★ Dc in each st across to ch-2 sp, [(2 dc, ch 2, 2 dc) in next ch-2 sp, dc in each of next 6 sts, skip next 4 sts, dc in each of next 6 sts] 3 times, (2 dc, ch 2, 2 dc) in next ch-2 sp; rep from ★ 3 times, dc in each rem st; join with slip st in 3rd ch of ch-3; ch 3: 41 dc each straight side.

Rnds 22-24: Rep Rnd 21, 3 times, continuing to increase 4 dc each straight side each rnd: 53 dc each straight side. At end of last rnd, do not ch, drop white. With pink, ch 3.

Rnds 25-30: Rep Rnd 21, 6 times, continuing to increase 4 dc each straight side each rnd, and working 1 rnd with each color in same color sequence as Rnds 12-17: 77 dc each straight side. At end of last rnd, finish off.

Finishing:

Corner Square (make 24):

With smallest size hook and white, work same as Blanket thru Rnd 1; do not finish off.

Rnd 2: Slip st in each st to ch-2 sp, work same as Blanket Rnd 2. Square should measure approx $1^1/_2$" x $1\ ^1/_2$" With 2 squares wrong sides tog, sew thru **back loop only** from 2nd ch of ch-2 corner across one side to first ch of next ch-2 corner. Rep to join 6 squares as shown in **Diagram**. Sew joined squares in points of ripple on blanket thru **back loop only**, skipping ch-2 on lower points of squares which join in area of skipped sts on blanket, and using ch-2 on points of ripple in space where 3 squares join. Rep to fill rem 3 corners of blanket.

Diagram

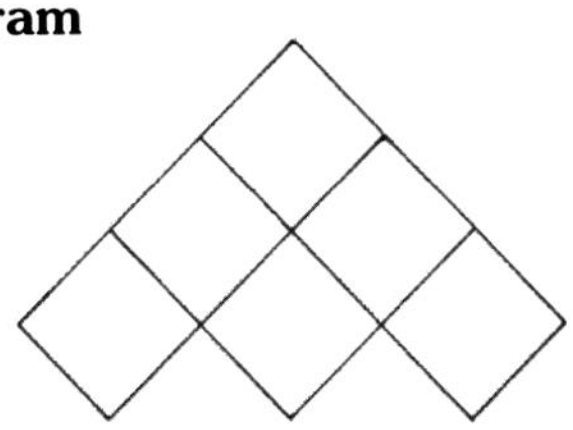

Edging

Rnd 1: Join white with slip st in any dc along straight side of blanket, ch 3, dc in each dc to next ch-2 point of ripple, ★ dec as follows: YO, pull up a loop in ch-2 sp on blanket, YO and draw thru 2 loops, YO, pull up a loop in ch-2 on first square of corner, YO and draw thru 2 loops, YO and draw thru all 3 loops on hook (dec made), (dc in each of next 7 sts, dec in next 2 ch-2 sps as before) twice, dc in each of next 7 sts, (2 dc, ch 2, 2 dc) in corner ch-2 sp, (dc in each of next 7 sts, dec in next 2 ch-2 sps) 3 times, dc in each dc to next ch-2 point of ripple on blanket; rep from ★ around, ending last rep dc in each rem dc; join with slip st in 3rd ch of ch-3, ch 3.

Rnd 2: ★ Dc in each st to next ch-2 corner, (2 dc, ch 2, 2 dc) in corner; rep from ★ 3 times, dc in each rem dc; join as before, ch 3.

Rnds 3 and 4: Rep Rnd 2 twice. At end of last rnd, join; do not ch; finish off.

Rnd 5: Join lt aqua with slip st in any dc along straight side of blanket, ch 3, rep Rnd 2. At end of rnd, do not ch; finish off. Weave in any yarn ends.

Jacket

Note: Yoke is worked in all right side rows.

Yoke:

With smaller size hook and pink, ch 59 loosely.

Row 1: Dc in 4th ch from hook, dc in next ch, ch 1, skip next 2 chs, 3 dc in next ch, ch 1, skip next 2 chs, † (3 dc, ch 2, 3 dc) in next ch, ch 1, (sk next 2 chs, 3 dc in next ch, ch 1) 3 times, skip next 2 chs, (3 dc, ch 2, 3 dc) in next ch, ch 1 †, (sk next 3 chs, 3 dc in next ch, ch 1) 3 times, skip next 3 chs; rep from † to † once, skip next 2 chs, 3 dc in next ch, ch 1, skip next 2 chs, dc in each of rem 3 chs; finish off: 21 dc clusters.

Row 2: Join apricot with slip st in 3rd ch of ch-3 at beg of prev row, ch 3, dc in next dc, (3 dc, ch 1) in each ch-1 sp to next ch-2 corner, ★ (3 dc, ch 2, 3 dc) in ch-2 sp, ch 1, (3 dc, ch 1) in each ch-1 sp to next ch-2 corner; rep from ★ twice, (3 dc, ch 2, 3 dc) in ch-2 sp, (ch 1, 3 dc) in each rem ch-1 sp, skip next dc, dc in each of rem 2 dc; finish off: 26 dc clusters.

Row 3: Join lt yellow in same manner as apricot, ch 3, dc in each of next 2 dc, skip next 2 dc, (ch 1, 3 dc) in each ch-1 sp to next ch-2 corner, ch 1, ★ (3 dc, ch 2, 3 dc) in ch-2 sp, ch 1, (3 dc, ch 1) in each ch-1 sp to next ch-2 corner; rep from ★ twice, (3 dc, ch 2, 3 dc) in next ch-2 sp, (ch 1, 3 dc) in each rem ch-1 sp, ch 1, skip next 2 dc, dc in each of rem 3 dc; finish off: 29 dc clusters.

Rows 4-6: Rep Rows 2 and 3 once, then rep Row 2 once more working 1 row each of the following colors: lt green, lt aqua, and lt lavender: 42 dc clusters.

Left Sleeve:

Join white with slip st in first ch-2 sp at side of yoke.

Row 1: Ch 3, skip next 2 dc, 3 hdc in next dc, ★ skip next 2 sts, 3 hdc in next st; rep from ★ 11 times, dc in ch-2 corner sp; ch 3, turn.

Row 2: Skip first 2 sts, 3 hdc in next hdc, ★ skip next 2 hdc, 3 hdc in next hdc; rep from ★ across, dc in ch-3 sp; ch 3, turn.

Rows 3-7: Rep Row 2, 5 times. At end of last row, do not ch; finish off.

Edging: Row 1: With piece right side facing, join pink with slip st in first st on last row of sleeve, ch 1, sc in same st as joining, sc in each st across; finish off.

Rows 2-6: Rep Row 1, 5 times in same color sequence as Rows 2-6 of Yoke.

Right Sleeve: Turn yoke with worked sleeve at bottom; join white with slip st in ch-2 sp in upper right corner of yoke. Work same as Left Sleeve.

Body: Join white with slip st in 3rd ch of ch-3 at beg of Row 6 on Yoke.

Row 1: Ch 3, (sk next 2 sts, 3 hdc in next st) 6 times, skip next 2 sts, 3 hdc in ch-2 corner sp, fold yoke so corner of front of yoke touches corner of back of yoke, 3 hdc in ch-2 corner sp on back of yoke, (sk next 2 sts, 3 hdc in next st) 12 times, skip next 3 sts, 3 hdc in ch-2 corner sp, fold yoke as before, 3 hdc in ch-2 corner sp on front of yoke, (sk next 2 sts, 3 hdc in next st) 6 times, skip next 2 sts, dc in rem st; ch 3, turn.

Rows 2-18: Rep Left Sleeve Row 2, 17 times. At end of last row, do not ch; finish off.

Finishing: Weave in any yarn ends. Sew sleeve seams.

Front Edging: With piece right side facing and neck edge at top, join white with slip st in lower right front corner; ch 2. Working around front edge, 2 hdc in end of each row to last row before neck edge, adjusting as necessary to make edging lie flat, skip end of last row, work (3 hdc, ch 2, 3 hdc) in unused loop of beg ch on foundation ch, 3 hdc in ch sp between each 3-dc group around entire neck edge, (3 hdc, ch 2, 3 hdc) in first ch of ch-3 at end of first row on yoke, work left front edge same as right front edge to lower corner; finish off. Cut 4, 9" lengths of ribbon. Sew one ribbon each side of neck edge and one ribbon each side of last row of yoke for ties.

Bootie (make 2):

Sole: With white, ch 13.

Rnd 1: Work 2 sc in 2nd ch from hook, sc in each of next 10 chs, 4 sc in last ch (toe), working other side of beg ch, sc in each of next 10 chs, 2 sc in last ch: 28 sc. Do not join rnds.

Rnd 2: Sc in first sc, mark this sc with contrasting yarn, moving marker to beg sc of each rnd, sc in same st (inc made), inc in next st, sc in each of next 9 sc, hdc in next sc, 2 dc in each of next 4 sc, hdc in next sc, sc in each of next 9 sc, inc in each of next 2 sc: 36 sts.

Rnd 3: Inc in first sc, sc in each of next 9 sc, hdc in next sc, dc in each of next 3 sts, hdc in each of next 3 dc, 2 hdc in each of next 2 dc, hdc in each of next 3 dc, dc in each of next 3 sts, hdc in next sc, sc in each of next 9 sc, inc in last sc: 40 sts.

Rnd 4: Inc in each of first 2 sc, sc in each of next 17 sts, inc in each of next 2 hdc, sc in each of next 17 sts, inc in each of next 2 sc, slip st in first sc; finish off.

Top:

With white, ch 4; join with slip st in beg ch to form ring.

Rnd 1: Ch 3, 2 dc in ring, ch 2, (3 dc in ring, ch 2) 3 times, slip st in 3rd ch of beg ch-3, ch 23 (heel), skip next 2 dc; being careful to not twist ch, join with slip st in next ch-2 sp: 11 dc.

Rnd 2: Ch 3, 2 dc in same ch-2 sp, (dc in each of next 3 dc, 4 dc in next ch-2 sp) twice, dc in each of next 3 dc, 3 dc in next ch-2 sp, dc in each of next 23 chs; join with slip st in 3rd ch of beg ch-3: 45 dc.

Rnd 3: Ch 1, sc in each dc around; finish off, leaving a 12" length for sewing. Turn Top inside out and place next to right side of Sole, matching sts, sew Sole and Top tog. Turn right side out.

Cuff:

Rnd 1 (Beading Rnd)**:** Join white with slip st in center dc of 3-dc group at toe, ch 3, dc in same st, ch 1, skip next dc, dc in next ch-2 sp, dc in next dc, ch 1, (sk next dc, dc in each of next 2 dc, ch 1) 7 times, dc in next ch-2 sp, dc in next dc, ch 1; join with slip st in 3rd ch of beg ch-3: 10 ch-1 sps.

Rnd 2: Ch 3, dc in each dc and ch-1 sp around; join with slip st in 3rd ch of beg ch-3; finish off: 29 dc.

Edging:

Rnd 1: Join pink with slip st in any dc at back of Booties, ch 1, sc in same st, sc in each st around; join with slip st in beg sc; finish off.

Rnds 2-6: Work in same manner as Rnd 1 in same color sequence as Rows 2-6 of Yoke of Jacket. Weave in any yarn ends. Cut 2 satin ribbons, each 18" long to weave thru ch-1 sps of Beading Rnd. Tie bow at center front.

Crocheted CHRISTENING SET

DRESS & BONNET

SIZE: Birth to 3 mos (to 13 lbs)

Dress Measurements:

chest	17"
length to underarm	17"
sleeve length	3"

MATERIALS: 4 balls (approx 200 yds each) bedspread wt cotton thread or baby wt yarn, 5 oz (142 grams) white; steel crochet hook size 4 (1.9 mm) or size needed for gauge; 3 1/2 yds (1/4") white satin ribbon; 3 (1/4") white buttons.

GAUGE: In dc, 7 sts = 1"; 4 rows = 1"
In double picot st patt, 6 sts = 4"; 5 rows = 2"

INSTRUCTIONS

Rose Motif:

First Motif: Ch 5, join with slip st in beg ch to form a ring.

Rnd 1: Ch 6, (dc in ring, ch 3) 5 times; join with slip st in 3rd ch of ch-6.

Rnd 2: ★ (Sc, hdc, 3 dc, hdc, sc) in next ch-3 loop; rep from ★ around.

Rnd 3: Sc around post of first petal ***(Fig. A)***, (ch 5, sc around post of next petal) 5 times, ch 5; join with slip st in beg sc.

Fig. A

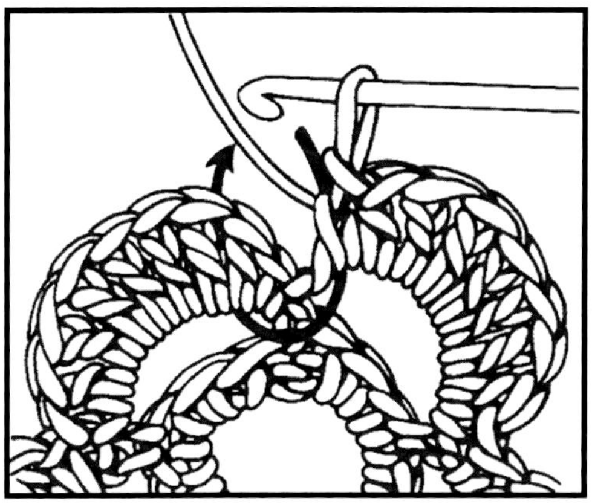

Rnd 4: ★ (Sc, hdc, 5 dc, hdc, sc) in next ch-5 loop; rep from ★ around.

Rnd 5: Rep Rnd 3, working ch 7 between each sc.

Rnd 6: ★ (Sc, dc, 7 tr, dc, sc) in next ch-7 loop; rep from ★ around; join with slip st in beg sc; finish off.

Rnd 7: Join thread with slip st in center tr on any petal, ch 1, sc in same st as joining, ch 7, † ★ YO, insert hook in last tr on same petal and pull up a loop, YO and draw thru 2 loops, YO, insert hook in first tr on next petal and pull up a loop, YO and draw thru 2 loops, YO and draw thru rem 3 loops, ch 7 †, sc in center tr on same petal, ch 7; rep from ★ 4 times, then rep from † to † once; join with slip st in beg sc.

Rnd 8: Slip st into next ch-7 sp, work beg cluster st as follows: ch 3, keeping last loop of each st on hook, work 2 dc in same sp, YO and draw thru all 3 loops at once (beg cluster st made), ch 9, work cluster st as follows: keeping last loop of each st on hook, work 3 dc in same ch-7 sp, YO and draw thru all 4 loops at once (cluster st made), † ★ (ch 7, sc in next ch-7 sp, ch 3, sc in same sp) twice, ch 7 †, (cluster st, ch 9, cluster st) in next ch-7 sp; rep from ★ twice, then work from † to † once; join with slip st in 3rd ch of beg ch-3; finish off.

2nd Motif: Work same as First Motif thru Rnd 7.

Rnd 8 (joining rnd)**:** Slip st into next ch-7 sp, work beg cluster st, ch 4, sc in center of ch-9 between cluster sts on one corner of first motif, ch 4, work cluster st in same ch-7 sp on 2nd motif, (ch 3, sc in next ch-7 sp on first motif, ch 3, sc in next ch-7 sp on 2nd motif, ch 3, sc in same sp on 2nd motif) twice, ch 3, sc in next ch-7 sp of first motif, ch 3, work cluster st in next ch-7 sp on 2nd motif, ch 4, sc in center of ch-9 on next corner on first motif, ch 4, work cluster st in same ch-7 sp on 2nd motif, complete Rnd 8 same as First Motif. Work 8 more motifs and join same as 2nd Motif to form straight strip 10 motifs long.

11th Motif: Work same as First Motif thru Rnd 7.

Rnd 8 (joining rnd)**:** Work same as 2nd Motif Rnd 8 to join 2 corners and one side, † (ch 7, sc in next ch-7 sp on 11th motif, ch 3, sc in same sp) twice, ch 7 †, taking care not to twist strip, join corner, 3rd side and rem corner of 11th Motif to corner, side and corner of First Motif; rep from † to † along rem side of 11th Motif; join with slip st in top of beg cluster st; finish off.

Note: Joined circle of motifs will be skirt edging.

Dress: Yoke: Ch 60 loosely. **Row 1:** Dc in 4th ch from hook and in each of next 4 chs, (2 dc, ch 1, 2 dc) in next ch, dc in each of next 13 chs, (2 dc, ch 1, 2 dc) in next ch, dc in each of next 16 chs, (2 dc, ch 1, 2 dc) in next ch, dc in each of next 13 chs, (2 dc, ch 1, 2 dc) in next ch, dc in each of rem 6 chs; ch 3, turn: 70 dc.

Row 2: Dc in each dc to ch-1 sp, (2 dc, ch 1, 2 dc) in ch-1 sp, dc in each of next 9 dc, (ch 3, skip next 2 dc, dc in next dc) twice, ch 3, skip 2 dc, (dc, ch 3, dc) in corner ch-1 sp, (ch 3, skip next 2 dc, dc in next dc) 6 times, ch 3, skip 2 dc, (dc, ch 3, dc) in corner ch-1 sp, (ch 3, skip next 2 dc, dc in next dc) 3 times, dc in each rem dc, working (2 dc, ch 1, 2 dc) in corner ch-1 sp; ch 3, turn: 56 dc.

Row 3: Dc in each dc to ch-1 corner, (2 dc, ch 1, 2 dc) in corner ch-1 sp, dc in each dc to mesh pattern, ch 3, skip first ch-3 sp, (dc in next ch-3 sp, ch 3) twice, (dc, ch 3, dc) in corner ch-3 sp, (ch 3, dc in next ch-3 sp) to next corner, ch 3, (dc, ch 3, dc) in corner ch-3 sp, (ch 3, dc in next ch-3 sp) twice, ch 3, skip rem ch-3 sp, dc in next dc and in each rem dc, working (2 dc, ch 1, 2 dc) in rem ch-1 corner sp; ch 3, turn: 65 dc.

Row 4: Dc in each dc to ch-1 corner, (2 dc, ch 1, 2 dc) in corner ch-1 sp, dc in each dc to mesh pattern, ch 3, dc in first ch-3 sp, ch 3, (dc in next ch-3 sp, ch 3) twice, (dc, ch 3, dc) in corner ch-3 sp, (ch 3, dc in next ch-3 sp) to next corner, ch 3, (dc, ch 3, dc) in corner ch-3 sp, (ch 3, dc in next ch-3 sp) twice, ch 3, dc in rem ch-3 sp, ch 3, dc in next dc and in each rem dc, working (2 dc,ch 1, 2 dc) in rem ch-1 corner sp; ch 3, turn: 76 dc.

Rows 5, 7 and 9: Having 1 more mesh sp between ch-3 corners each row, work in same manner as Row 3, 3 times.

Rows 6 and 8: Having 1 more mesh sp between dc patt and ch-3 corners and 1 more mesh sp between ch-3 corners each row, work in same manner as Row 4, twice. At end of Row 9, you should have 125 dc.

Row 10 (joining row)**:** Dc in each dc to first ch-1 corner, 2 dc in ch-1 corner, ch 7, fold yoke so corner just worked touches next ch-3 corner, 2 dc in ch-3 corner, dc in next dc, ★ 2 dc in next ch-3 sp, dc in next dc; rep from ★ to next ch-3 corner, 2 dc in ch-3 corner, ch 7, fold yoke as before, 2 dc in ch-1 corner, dc in each rem dc; join with slip st in 3rd ch of beg ch-3; ch 3, turn: 113 sts.

Skirt

Rnd 1: Dc in each st around; join with slip st in 3rd ch of ch-3; do not turn: 113 dc.

Rnd 2 (beading rnd)**:** Ch 4, dc in 2nd dc, ch 1, skip next dc, ★ dc in next dc, ch 1 skip next dc; rep from ★ to last dc, dc in last dc, ch 1; join with slip st in 3rd ch of beg ch-4: 58 ch-1 sps.

Rnd 3: Ch 3, ★ dc in next ch-1 sp, dc in next dc; rep from ★ around; join with slip st in 3rd ch of beg ch-3: 116 dc.

Rnd 4: Work double picot st as follows: (ch 4, slip st in 3rd ch from hook) twice, ch 1 (double picot st made), skip next dc, sc in next dc, (work double picot st, skip next dc, sc in next dc) 3 times, (work double picot st, skip next 2 dc, sc in next dc) 14 times, (work double picot st, skip next dc, sc in next dc) 8 times, (work double picot st, skip next 2 dc, sc in next dc) 14 times, (work double picot st, skip next dc, sc in next dc) 3 times, work double picot st, skip next dc; join with slip st in next sc: 44 double picot sts.

Rnd 5: Work double picot st, sc in center of next double picot st, mark stitch just worked for beg of rnd, ★ work double picot st, sc in center of next double picot st; rep from ★ around. Moving marker each rnd rep Rnd 5 until 33 double picot st rnds have been worked.

(***Note:*** Skirt should measure approx 13½" from Beading Rnd). At end of last rnd, sc in center of marked st.

Skirt Edging

Joining Rnd: With both pieces right side facing, hold circle of joined rose motifs above bottom edge of skirt. Ch 3, ★ sc in sc joining between 2 motifs on skirt edging, (ch 3, sc in center of next double picot st on skirt, ch 3, sc in next ch-7 sp on edging) 3 times, ch 3, sc in center of next double picot st on skirt, ch 3; rep from ★ around, ending last rep slip st in first ch of beg ch-3; finish off. Join yarn on opposite edge of motifs with slip st in sc joining between 2 motifs.

Last Rnd: Ch 5, (tr, ch 3, slip st in 3rd ch from hook to form picot, 2 tr) in same st, ★ ch 4, (sc, ch 3, sc) in next ch-7 sp, ch 4, (2 tr, picot, 2 tr) in 4th ch of next ch-7 sp, ch 4, (sc, ch 3, sc) in next ch-7 sp, ch 4, (2 tr, picot, 2 tr) in sc joining between next 2 motifs; rep from ★ around, ending last rep slip st in 5th ch of beg ch-5; finish off.

Left Sleeve

With piece right side facing, join yarn with slip st in center ch of ch-3 corner on left front.

Rnd 1: Work double picot st as follows: (ch 4, slip st in 3rd ch from hook) twice, ch 1 (double picot st made), sc in next dc, (work double picot st, skip next ch-3 sp, sc in next dc) 6 times, (work double picot st, skip next 3 dc, sc in next dc) 6 times, work double picot st, skip end of next row and unused loop of next ch (of ch-7), sc in unused loop of next ch, work double picot st, skip next 3 sts, sc in unused loop of next ch, work double picot st, sc in center of beg double picot st; mark last st worked: 16 double picot sts.

Rnd 2: Work double picot st, sc in center of next double picot st, mark stitch just worked for beg of rnd, ★ work double picot st, sc in center of next double picot st; rep from ★ around.

Rnds 3-6: Rep Rnd 2, 4 times.

Rnd 7: ★ Ch 2, sc in center of next double picot st; rep from ★ around; join with slip st in first ch of beg ch-2.

Rnd 8: Ch 4, ★ dc in next sc, ch 1; rep from ★ around; join with slip st in 3rd ch of beg ch-4; finish off: 16 sps.

Right Sleeve

With piece right side facing, join yarn with slip st in dc to left of ch-1 corner on back of yoke.

Rnd 1: Work double picot st as follows: (ch 4, slip st in 3rd ch from hook) twice, ch 1 (double picot st made), skip next 3 dc, sc in next dc, (work double picot st, skip next 3 dc, sc in next dc) 5 times, (work double picot st, skip next ch-3 sp, sc in next dc) 6 times, work double picot st, skip end of next row and unused loop of next ch (of ch-7), sc in unused loop of next ch, work double picot st, skip next 3 sts, sc in unused loop of next ch, work double picot st, sc in center of beg double picot st; mark last st worked: 16 sts.

Rnds 2-8: Work same as Left Sleeve.

Large Leaf (make 2)

Row 1: Ch 15, sc in 2nd ch from hook and in each of next 12 chs, 3 sc in end ch, working in unused loop of each ch, sc in each of next 11 chs, leave rem 2 chs unworked; ch 2, turn.

Row 2: Skip first 2 sc, working in **back loop only** (now and throughout), sc in each of next 10 sc, 3 sc in next sc, sc in each of next 12 sc, leave rem 2 sc unworked; ch 2, turn.

Row 3: Skip first 2 sc, sc in each of next 11 sc, 3 sc in next sc, sc in each of next 11 sc; ch 2, turn.

Row 4: Skip first 2 sc, sc in each of next 10 sc, 3 sc in next sc, sc in each of next 12 sc; ch 2, turn.

Row 5: Rep Row 3; at end of row, do not ch; finish off.

Small Leaf (make 2)

Row 1: Ch 9, sc in 2nd ch from hook and in each of next 6 chs, 3 sc in end ch, working in unused loop of each ch, sc in each of next 6 chs, leave rem ch unworked; ch 2, turn.

Row 2: Skip first 2 sc, working in **back loop only** (now and throughout), sc in each of next 5 sc, 3 sc in next sc, sc in each of next 7 sc, leave rem sc unworked; ch 2, turn.

Row 3: Skip first 2 sc, sc in each of next 6 sc, 3 sc in next sc, sc in each of next 5 sc, leave rem sc unworked; ch 2, turn.

Row 4: Skip first 2 sc, sc in each of next 4 sc, 3 sc in next sc, sc in each of next 6 sc; finish off.

Small Rose (make 2)

Work same as Rose Motif thru Rnd 4. At end of last rnd, join with slip st in beg sc; finish off.

Center Rose

Work same as Rose Motif thru Rnd 6.

Finishing

Refer to photo (**pg. 12**) and **Diagram** for placement of roses and leaves on front of yoke. Sew each piece to mesh background. Cut 2, 18" lengths of white ribbon. Beginning at top of sleeve, thread ribbon thru Beading Rnd working over 1 dc and under next dc. Cut 54" length of ribbon and thread thru Beading Rnd on dress in same manner, tie a bow in front and trim ends to desired length. Using sp between last 2 dc on row for buttonhole, sew button on end of Rows 1, 4 and 7 on yoke.

Diagram

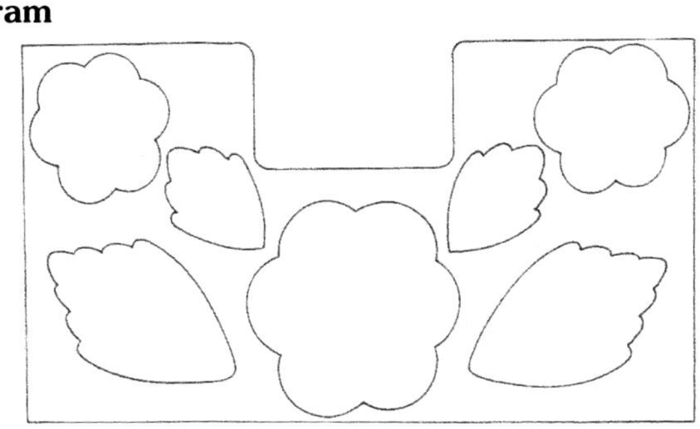

Bonnet

Work and join 3 Rose Motifs in straight strip same as for Skirt.

Back: Work 4th Rose Motif thru Rnd 7.

Rnd 8: Slip st in each of first 3 chs of next ch-7 sp, ch 1, work 4 sc in same sp, sc in next sc, work 7 sc in next ch-7 sp, sc in next sc, work 3 sc in next ch-7 sp, sc in center ch of same ch-7, (work double picot st, sc in next ch-7 sp) 3 times, (work double picot st, sc in next ch-7 sp, work double picot st, sc in same sp) 3 times, (work double picot st, sc in next ch-7 sp) 3 times, work double picot st; join with slip st in beg sc; turn.

Crown

Row 1: Slip st to center of first picot, skip center of same st, (work double picot st, sc in center of next double picot st) 12 times, slip st to center of last picot; turn.

Row 2: (Work double picot st, sc in center of next double picot st) 12 times, slip st to center of last picot; turn.

Row 3: Rep Row 2.

Row 4 (joining row)**:** Ch 3, sc in center ch of ch-9 between cluster sts on motif strip, ★ † (ch 3, sc in center of next double picot st on bonnet, ch 3, sc in next ch-7 sp on motif) 3 times, ch 3, sc in center of next double picot st on bonnet †, ch 3, sc in sc joining between motifs; rep from ★ once, then rep from † to † once, slip st to center of next picot on bonnet, ch 3, sc in center of ch of rem ch-9 corner; finish off. Join yarn on opposite edge of motifs with slip st in center ch of ch-9 corner. Work edging across front edge only of bonnet same as Last Rnd on Skirt Edging; finish off.

Beading Row

With right side of Bonnet facing and bottom edge at top, join with slip st in base of last tr of front edging, ch 5, (dc in ch-7 sp, ch 2) 5 times, (dc in next picot, ch 2) twice, (sk 3 sc, dc in next sc, ch 2) 3 times, (dc in next picot, ch 2) twice, (dc in next ch-7 sp, ch 2) 5 times, ending by working a dc in base of beg ch-5 of front edging; finish off: 18 sps. Cut 30" length of ribbon. Thread thru Beading Row on neck edge of bonnet. Leaving 9" each side for ties, sew ribbon to corner of bonnet each side.

Crocheted
LOVE KNOT SET

DRESS & BONNET

SIZES:	**12 mos**	**24 mos**
Approx weight:	to 24 lbs	to 30 lbs
Body Chest:	20"	21"
Garment Measurements:		
chest	21"	22"
skirt length	$8^{1}/_{2}$"	$9^{1}/_{2}$"

Size Note: Instructions are written for smaller size with changes for larger size in parentheses.

MATERIALS: Baby wt yarn, 3 oz (85.2 grams) white, 1 oz (28.4 grams) peach; steel crochet hook size 2 (2.10 mm) or size needed for gauge; 2½ yds ($^{1}/_{4}$") peach satin ribbon; 3 ($^{1}/_{4}$") white buttons.

GAUGE: In dc, 5 sts = 1"; 5 rows = 2"

Pattern Stitch

For practice swatch, ch 21 loosely.

Row 1: ★ Make a double knot st as follows: pull up loop on hook to measure $^{1}/_{2}$", YO and draw thru (loose ch made), sc in **back loop only** ***(Fig. A)*** of loose ch just made, pull up loop now on hook to measure $^{1}/_{2}$" ***(Fig. B)***, YO and draw thru, sc in back loop only ***(Fig. C)*** of loose ch just made (double knot st made), skip next 2 chs, sc in next ch; rep from ★ across: 7 knot sts. To turn, work loose ch, sc in **back loop only** of loose ch just made (single knot st made and this becomes turning leg); turn.

Row 2: Work double knot st, sc in center of first double knot st ***(Fig. D)***, ★ work double knot st, sc in center of next double knot st; rep from ★ across; turn as before. Rep Row 2 for patt. ***Fig. E*** shows completed Love Knot St. Work a total of 8 rows for a practice swatch. Piece should measure approx 4" x 4".

Fig. A

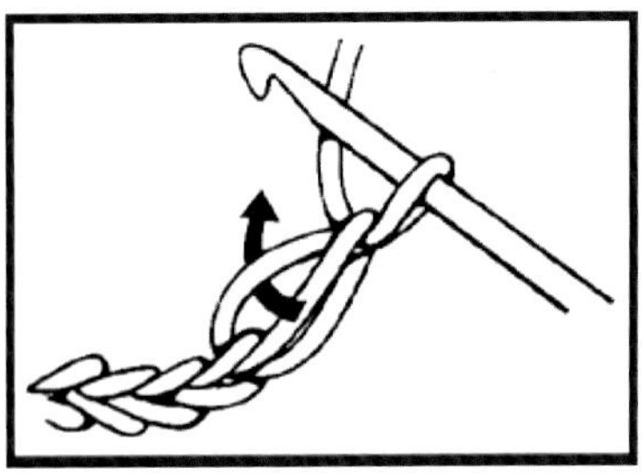

Fig. B

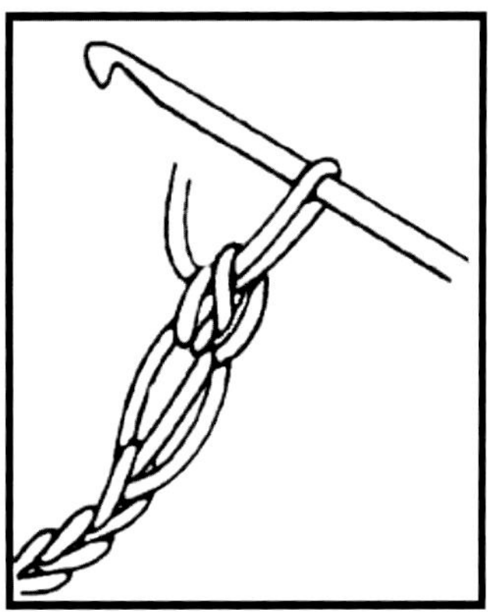

Fig. C

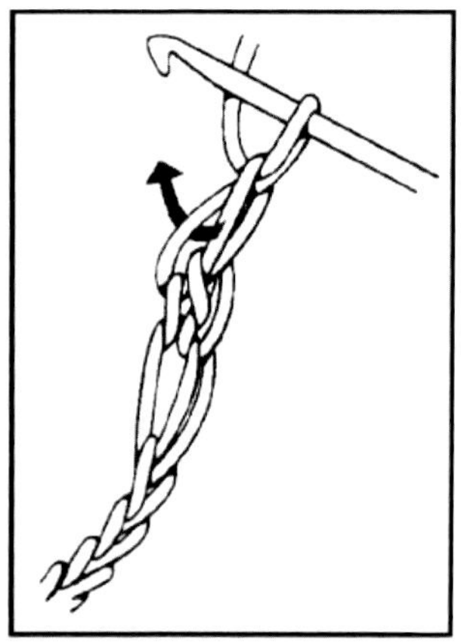

Fig. D

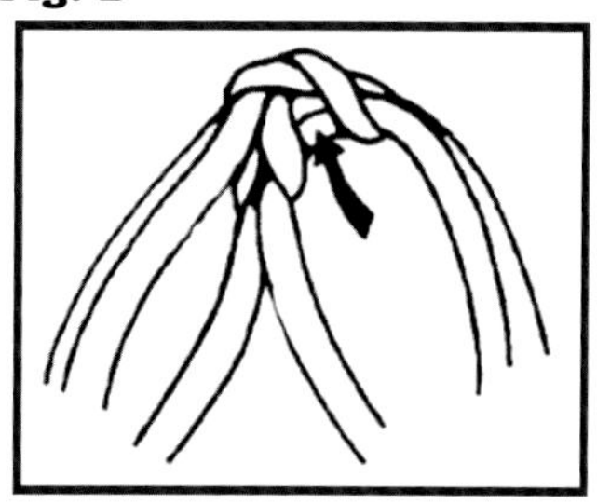

Fig. E

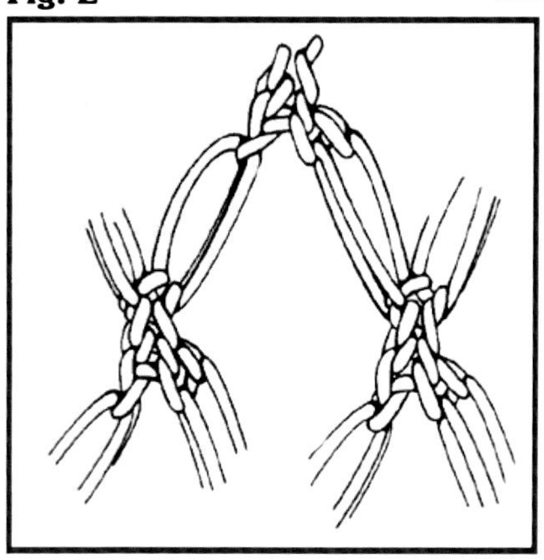

INSTRUCTIONS

Dress: Yoke: With white, ch 57(73) loosely.

Note: Ch-3 (turning ch) counts as dc throughout.

Row 1 (right side)**:** Dc in 4th ch from hook and in each of next 4(6) chs, ★ (2 dc, ch 1, 2 dc) in next ch, dc in each of next 13(17) chs; rep from ★ twice, (2 dc, ch 1, 2 dc) in next ch, dc in each of rem 6(8) chs; ch 3, turn.

Row 2: ★ Dc in each dc to next ch-1 sp, work corner as follows: (2 dc, ch 1. 2 dc) in ch-1 sp (corner made); rep from ★ 3 times, dc in each rem dc; ch 3, turn.

Row 3: Rep Row 2; at end of row, ch 4, turn.

Row 4 (beading row)**:** Skip next dc, (dc in next dc, ch 1, skip next dc) 5(6) times, ★ work corner, ch 1, skip next dc, (dc in next dc, ch 1, skip next dc) 12(14) times; rep from ★ twice, work corner, (ch 1, skip next dc, dc in next dc) 6(7) times; ch 3, turn.

Row 5: ★ Dc in each dc and in each ch-1 sp to comer, work corner; rep from ★ 3 times, dc in each rem dc and ch-1 sp; ch 3, turn.

Rows 6 and 7: Rep Row 2 twice. At end of last row, join yoke at center back with slip st in 3rd ch of ch-3 at beg of last row; finish off. ***Note:*** Open ends of Rows 1-7 form back neck opening.

Underarm Opening

With right side facing, join white with slip st in ch-1 corner to left of back opening, ch 10; join with slip st in next ch-1 corner sp on yoke ***(Diagram)***; finish off. Rep to join rem 2 corners.

Diagram

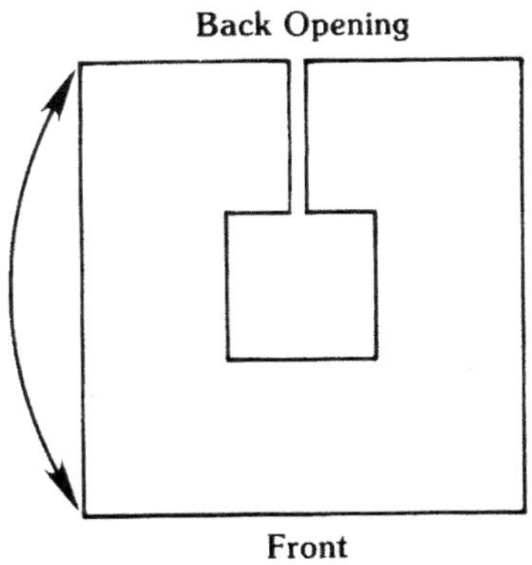

Skirt

Rnd 1 (beading rnd)**:** Join white with slip st in center back joining; ch 4, skip next dc, dc in next dc, (ch 1, skip next dc, dc in next dc) 8(9) times, ch 1, skip next dc, dc in next ch, (ch 1, skip next ch, dc in next ch) 4 times, ch 1, skip next ch, dc in next dc, (ch 1, skip next dc, dc in next dc) 20(22) times, (ch 1, skip next ch, dc in next ch) 5 times, (ch 1, skip next dc, dc in next dc) 10(11) times; join with slip st in 3rd ch of beg ch-3, ch 1.

Rnd 2: Sc in same st as joining, ★ skip next ch-1 sp, (2 dc, ch 1, 2 dc) in next dc, skip next ch-1 sp, sc in next dc; rep from ★ around, ending last rep slip st in beg sc.

Rnd 3: Refer to Pattern Stitch for instructions and ★ work double knot st, sc in next ch-1 sp, work double knot st, sc in next sc; rep from ★ around, work double knot st; join with slip st in slip st joining of prev rnd. Do not turn.

Rnd 4: Work loose ch same as in Pattern Stitch, slip st in center of next double knot st, ★ work double knot st, sc in center of next double knot st; rep from ★ around, ending by working double knot st; join with slip st in slip st at beg of rnd, **turn**. Rep Rnd 4 until skirt measures approx 8(9)" from beading rnd. At end of last rnd, finish off white; turn.

Edging

Join peach with slip st in center of last double knot st on prev rnd; sc in same sp as joining, ★ work double knot st, sc in center of next double knot st; rep from ★ around, work double knot st; join with slip st in sc at beg of rnd; finish off.

Finishing

Note: Row 1 of Yoke Ruffle is worked in top of sts on Row 4 (beading row) and thru base of sts on Row 5 of yoke.

Yoke Ruffle

Hold piece right side of back facing and with neck edge at bottom.

Row 1: Join white with slip st in dc at beg of beading row on yoke, sc in same st, working around yoke, (work double knot st, skip next ch-1 sp, sc in top of next dc) 6(7) times, work corner as follows: work double knot st, skip next dc, sc in center of corner, work double knot st, skip next dc, sc in next dc (corner made), ★ (work double knot st, sc in next dc) 14(15) times, work corner as before; rep from ★ twice, (work double knot st, sc in top of next dc) 5(6) times, work double knot st, sc in 3rd ch of ch-4 on beading rnd; work double knot st, turn.

Row 2: ★ Sc in center of next double knot st, work double knot st; rep from ★ to last st, sc in center of last double knot st; finish off; turn.

Row 3: Join peach with slip st in center of first double knot st on Row 1, ch 1, sc in same st as joining, ★ work double knot st, sc in center of next double knot st on Row 2; rep from ★ around; finish off.

Armhole Ruffle

Row 1: Join white with slip st in first dc to left of ch-1 corner sp on last row of left front yoke, ch 1, sc in same st as joining, ★ work double knot st, skip next dc, sc in next dc; rep from ★ to last dc before next ch-1 corner, work double knot st, skip rem dc, sc in ch-1 corner sp on yoke; turn.

Row 2: Work loose ch, sc in center of next double knot st, ★ work double knot st, sc in center of next double knot st; rep from ★ across, (work double knot st, skip ch-1 sp on underarm, sc in top of next dc) 5 times, ★ ★ work double knot st, sc in center of next double knot st; rep from ★ ★ across to first double knot st on underarm, work double knot st, sc in center of first double knot st on underarm; finish off; turn.

Edging

Work same as Skirt Edging. Work ruffle around opposite armhole in same manner. Cut approx 24(26)" length of ribbon. Beginning at center back, thread ribbon under first dc of yoke beading row, over next dc and under next dc; continue in same manner around entire yoke working over 2 dc in each corner sp. Distribute ribbon evenly around; trim any excess. Turn under approx 1/4" each end and sew one end to each side of back opening. Cut approx 33(35)" length of ribbon and beginning and ending at center front, thread thru skirt beading rnd, working under 1 dc and over 2 dc. Tie in bow at center front. Weave in any yarn ends. Using sp between last 2 dc on row for buttonhole, sew button on beg of Rows 1, 3 and 5 on yoke.

Bonnet

Beginning at center back, with white, ch 13(17) loosely.

Row 1 (wrong side)**:** Dc in 4th ch from hook and in each ch to last ch, 7 dc in rem ch, turn piece to work along opposite side, dc in unused loop of each ch across; ch 3, turn: 27(35) dc.

Row 2 (right side)**:** Dc in each of next 9(13) dc, 2 dc in each of next 7 dc, dc in each of rem 10(14) dc; turn: 34(42) dc.

Row 3: Refer to Pattern Stitch for instructions and work double knot st, sc in 2nd dc, ★ work double knot st, skip next dc, sc in next dc; rep from ★ across; work turning leg, turn, slip st in center of last double knot st on prev row.

Row 4: ★ Work double knot st, sc in center of next double knot st; rep from ★ across, turn.

Row 5: Work double knot st, ★ sc in center of next double knot st, work double knot st; rep from ★ across; sc in top of turning leg, work double knot st, turn, sc in center of last double knot st on prev row.

Row 6: Rep Row 4.

Row 7: Work loose ch, slip st in center of first double knot st, ch 1, sc in same st, ★ ch 4, sc in center of next double knot st; rep from ★ across; ch 1, turn.

Row 8: Sc in first sc, ★ 4 sc in next ch-4 sp, sc in next sc; rep from ★ across; turn.

Row 9: Work in same manner as Row 3, working into every 5th sc.

Rows 10-14: Rep Row 4, 5 times.

Row 15: Rep Row 7.

Row 16: Rep Row 8; at end of row, ch 4, turn.

Row 17 (beading row)**:** Skip next sc, dc in next sc, ★ ch 1, skip next sc, dc in next sc; rep from ★ across; ch 1, turn.

Row 18: Sc in each dc and ch-1 sp across, ending by working sc in each of next 2 chs of ch-4; turn.

Next 2(3) Rows: Rep Row 3, 2(3) times. At end of last row, sc in each st across bottom; finish off.

Edging

Work same as Skirt Edging. Cut 33(35)" length of ribbon. Thread thru beading row in same manner as ribbon on skirt. Sew ribbon to edge of bonnet on each side. Weave in any yarn ends.

Crocheted CARDIGAN

SIZES:	**6 mos**	**12 mos**	**24 mos**
Approx weight:	to 18 lbs	to 24 lbs	to 30 lbs
Body Chest:	19 1/2"	20"	21"
Garment Measurements:			
chest	20"	21"	22"
length to underarm	5 1/2"	6 1/2"	7 1/2"
sleeve length	6 1/2"	7 1/2"	8"

Size Note: Instructions are written in smallest size with changes for larger sizes in parentheses.

MATERIALS: Baby wt yarn, 3(3-4) oz [approx 85.2 (85.2-113.6) grams] white, 1 oz (28.4 grams) blue; aluminum crochet hooks size F (3.75 mm), and **for Sleeve Ribbing only** size D (3.25 mm), or sizes needed for gauge; 6 (½") buttons.

GAUGE: In patt, 14 hdc = 3"; 11 rows = 3"
In ribbing, 6 sc = 1"; 5 rows =1"

Pattern Stitch
For practice, ch 16 loosely.

Row 1: Hdc in 3rd ch from hook and in each ch across; ch 2, turn: 14 hdc. ***Note:*** Ch-2 (turning ch) does not count as a st.

Row 2: Work beg cross stitch as follows: skip first hdc, hdc in next hdc, sc loosely in skipped hdc ***Fig A,*** (beg cross stitch made), ★ work cross stitch as follows: skip next hdc, hdc in next hdc, sc loosely in skipped hdc (cross stitch made); rep from ★ across; ch 2, turn: 7 cross stitches.

Row 3: Hdc in first st and in each st across; ch 2, turn: 14 hdc. Rep Rows 2 and 3, 4 times. Piece should measure approx 3" x 3".

Fig. A

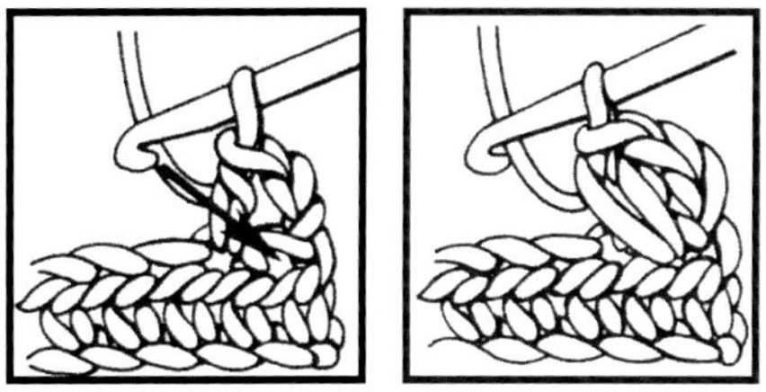

INSTRUCTIONS
Note: Garment is worked in one piece to underarm.

Body
With larger size hook and white, ch 92(98-104) loosely.

Rows 1-3: Work Part Rows 1-3: 90(96-102) hdc. Mark Row 2 for right side of piece. Rep Rows 2 and 3 until piece measures approx 4(5-6)" or 1½" less than desired length to underarm (allowing 1½" for bottom ribbing to be worked later), ending by working Row 2.

Left Front
Row 1: Hdc in first st and in each of next 14(16-18) sts, dec as follows: YO, pull up a loop in each of next 2 sts, YO and draw thru all 4 loops on hook (dec made), hdc in next st; ch 2, turn, leaving rem sts unworked: 17(19-21) sts.

Row 2: Skip first hdc, work in est cross st across; ch 2, turn: 8(9-10) cross stitches.

Row 3: Hdc in each st across to last 3 sts, dec, hdc in rem st; ch 2, turn: 15(17-19) sts. Rep Rows 2 and 3, 2(3-3) times, then rep Row 2 once: 5(5-6) cross sts.

SIZE 24 mos ONLY
Row 11: Rep Row 3: 11 sts.

Row 12: Hdc in first st, work in est cross st across.

Row 13: Rep Row 3: 10 sts.

Row 14: Work in est cross st across: 5 cross sts.

ALL SIZES: At end of last row, finish off.

Back
With piece wrong side facing, skip 8 sts (4 cross sts) from last st on Row 1 of Left Front, join white with slip st in next st, ch 2.

Row 1: Hdc in same st as joining, dec, hdc in each of next 32(34-36) sts, dec, hdc in next st; ch 2, turn, leaving rem sts unworked: 36(38-40) sts.

Row 2: Skip first hdc, work in est cross st across to last st, leave rem st unworked; ch 2, turn: 17(18-19) cross sts.

Row 3: Hdc in first st, dec, hdc in each st across to last 3 sts, dec, hdc in rem st; ch 2, turn: 32(34-36) sts. Rep Rows 2 and 3, 2(3-3) times, then rep Row 2 once more: 11(10-11) cross sts.

SIZE 24 mos ONLY:
Row 11: Rep Row 3: 20 sts.

Row 12: Hdc in first st, work in est cross st across to last st, hdc in rem st.

Row 13: Rep Row 3: 18 sts.

Row 14: Work in est cross st across: 9 cross sts.

ALL SIZES: At end of last row, finish off.

Right Front: With piece wrong side facing, skip 8 sts from last st worked on Row 1 of back, join white with slip st in next st, ch 2.

Row 1: Hdc in same st as joining, dec, hdc in each rem st; ch 2, turn.

Row 2: Work in est cross st to last st, leave last st unworked; ch 2, turn.

Row 3: Hdc in first st, dec, hdc in each rem st; ch 2, turn. Work same as Left Front reversing all shaping.

Sleeve

With white, ch 36(38-40) loosely.

Rows 1-3: Work Patt Rows 1-3: 34(36-38) hdc. Mark Row 2 for right side of piece. Rep Rows 2 and 3 until piece measures approx 5½(6½-7)" or 1" less than desired length to underarm, ending by working Row 2. At end of last row, turn, slip st in each of next 4 sts, ch 2.

Raglan Shaping

Row 1: Hdc in next st, dec, hdc in each of next 20(22-24) sts, dec, hdc in next st; ch 1, turn, leaving rem sts unworked: 24(26-28) sts. Beginning with Row 2, work Rows 2 and 3 of Back until 6(7-8) rows have been worked and 6 cross sts remain. At end of last row, finish off white, turn. Join blue with slip st in first st, ch 1.

Top of Sleeve

Row 1: With blue, sc in **back loop only** (BLO) of each st across; ch 1, turn: 12 sc.

Row 2 (dec row)**:** Continuing to work in BLO throughout, sc in first sc, dec as follows: YO, pull up a loop in each of next 2 sts, YO and draw thru all 4 loops on hook (dec made), sc in each sc to last 3 sc, dec, sc in rem sc: 10 sc.

SIZE 6 mos ONLY: Rep Rows 1 and 2, twice: 6 sts.

SIZES 12 and 24 mos ONLY: Rep Row 1, 4 times, rep Row 2 once, then rep Row 1 once more: 8 sts.

ALL SIZES: At end of last row, finish off.

Finishing

With body right side facing and bottom edge at top, join blue with slip st in unused loop of beg ch, ch 9.

Bottom Ribbing

Rib Row 1: Sc in back ridge of 2nd ch from hook and in each rem ch across, slip st in each of next 2 sts on body ***(Fig. B)***; ch 1, turn: 8 sc.

Fig. B

Rib Row 2: Skip first 2 slip sts sc in BLO of each sc on prev rib row; ch 1, turn: 8 sc.

Rib Row 3: Sc in BLO of each sc across, slip st in each of next 2 sts on body; ch 1, turn. Rep Rib Rows 2 and 3 across lower edge of body, then rep Rib Row 2 once more. At end of last row, do not ch; finish off.

Sleeve Ribbing

Hold piece with sleeve right side facing and bottom edge at top; with smaller size hook, join blue with slip st in unused loop of beg ch, ch 7. Work same as Bottom Ribbing: 6 sc. Sew sleeve seams. Sew sleeves in armholes.

Neck Band

Join blue with slip st in corner hdc on Right Front, ch 1.

Row 1: Sc in each st to last st on Right Front, using last sc on Right Front and first sc on Sleeve, dec across seam, sc in each sc to last sc on Sleeve, dec across seam, sc in each st to last st on Back, dec across seam, sc in each sc to last sc on Sleeve, dec across seam, sc in each st on Left Front; ch 1, turn.

Rows 2-5: Working dec above each dec on prev row, sc in each sc across; ch 1, turn. At end of last row ch 1, turn piece slightly to work along Left Front edge.

Front Band

(Note: Instructions are written for buttonholes on both sides. You can then sew buttons over unused buttonholes, sewing buttonholes closed as you sew on buttons. The placement of buttons then determines whether your sweater will be for a girl or for a boy.)

Row 1: Work one sc in end of each row along Neck Band and front edge, then sc in each st of Bottom Ribbing, adjusting sts as necessary to keep Front Band flat; ch 1, turn.

Rows 2 and 3: Sc in each sc across; ch 1, turn. Mark placement for 6 evenly spaced buttonholes.

Row 4: Sc in each st across, working (ch 1, skip next sc) over each marked st; ch 1, turn.

Rows 5 and 6: Rep Rows 2 and 3; at end of last row, do not ch; finish off. Join blue in last sc on Bottom Ribbing on Right Front, ch 1. Work Front Band Rows 1-6 along Right Front edge. Sew on buttons; Weave in any yarn ends.

Knitted RIBBED SET

SWEATER, HAT & BOOTIES

SIZES:	**6 mos**	**12 mos**	**24 mos**
Approx weight:	to 18 lbs	to 24 lbs	to 30 lbs
Body Chest:	19 1/2"	20"	21"

Garment Measurements: ***Note:*** Pattern stitch is very elastic.

chest	17"	19"	20"
length to underarm	5 1/2"	6 1/2"	7 1/2"
sleeve length	6 1/2"	7 1/2"	8"

Size Note: Instructions are written in smallest size with changes for larger sizes in parentheses.

Note: Booties are written in size 6 mos only.

MATERIALS: Sport Wt Yarn - white

Set	8 oz (227.2 grams)
Sweater	4 oz (113.6 grams)
Hat	2 oz (56.8 grams)
Booties	2 oz (56.8 grams)

Straight knitting needles sizes 2 (2.75 mm) and 3 (3.25 mm) or sizes needed for gauge; **for Bootie Finishing only**, steel crochet hook size 1 (2.3 mm); 3 (1/2") buttons; tapestry or yarn needle; 1/2 yd (3/8") white satin ribbon.

GAUGE: With larger size needles in patt,
8 sts = 1"; 8 rows = 1"
With larger size needles in stock st,
7 sts = 1"; 8 rows = 1"

◇◇◇◇◇◇◇◇◇◇◇◇◇◇◇◇◇◇◇◇◇◇◇◇◇◇◇◇◇◇

Pattern Stitch

Row 1: ★ P2, K1, P1, K1; rep from ★ across to last 2 sts, P2.
Row 2: ★ K2, P3; rep from ★ across to last 2 sts, K2.

For practice, CO 32 sts. Work 32 rows; piece should measure 4" x 4" without stretching.

◇◇◇◇◇◇◇◇◇◇◇◇◇◇◇◇◇◇◇◇◇◇◇◇◇◇◇◇◇◇

INSTRUCTIONS

Sweater Back: With larger size needles, CO 67(77-82) sts loosely. Work Patt Rows 1 and 2. Rep Patt Rows 1 and 2 until piece measures approx 6(6$^1/_2$-7)" from beg, ending by working Patt Row 2.

Raglan Shaping: Continuing in est patt, BO 3(4-4) sts at beg of next 2 rows: 61(69-74) sts. Dec one st each side every row 14(18-16) times, then EOR 5(4-7) times. BO rem 23(25-28) sts.

Front: With larger size needles, CO 67(77-82) sts loosely. Work same as Back until piece measures approx 2(2$^1/_4$-2$^3/_4$)" from first armhole BO, ending by working Patt Row 2: 33(37-38) sts.

Neck Shaping: Continuing to work decs each side at armhole edge same as Back, work in est patt across 10(12-12) sts; attach a new ball of yarn and BO in patt next 13(13-14) sts, work in est patt across rem 9(11-11) sts: 10(12-12) sts each side. Working on both sides, work Patt Row 2 once.

SIZE 6 mos ONLY: Continuing in est patt, dec one st each side at armhole edge EOR 5 times AND AT THE SAME TIME dec one st each side of neck EOR 4 times; draw yarn thru rem st to finish off.

SIZE 12 mos ONLY: Continuing in est patt, dec one st each side at armhole edge each row twice, then dec one st each side at armhole edge EOR 4 times AND AT THE SAME TIME dec one st each side of neck EOR 4 times: 2 sts each side.

Next Row: P2 tog each side; draw yarn thru rem st to finish off.

SIZE 24 mos ONLY: Continuing in est patt, dec one st each side at armhole edge EOR 5 times AND AT THE SAME TIME dec one st each side of neck each row 3 times, then dec one st each side of neck EOR twice.

Next Row: P2 tog each side; draw yarn thru rem st to finish off.

Sleeve (make 2)
With larger size needles, CO 32(37-42) sts. Work Patt Rows 1 and 2, then rep Patt Rows 1 and 2 twice.

Next Row: Inc in first st, work in est Patt to last st, inc in last st: 34(39-44) sts.

(*Note:* Work inc sts in est part.)

Increasing one st each side every 6(6-9)th row, 5(6-5) times more, then inc at beg of next row 0(1-0) time(s), continue in est Patt until piece measures 6$^1/_2$(7$^1/_2$-8)" or desired length to undearm, ending by working Patt Row 2: 44(52-54) sts. Work raglan sleeve shaping same as Raglan Shaping for Back. Draw yarn thru rem st; finish off.

Finishing
With right sides tog, sew side seams and sleeve seams. Sew sleeves into armholes, leaving 2$^1/_2$(3-3)" open on left shoulder front. Starting at left shoulder of front with smaller size needles, pick up 53(55-57) sts along neck edge only.

Row 1: Work in K1, P1 rib across, end K1.

Row 2: Work in P1, K1 rib across, end P1.

Rows 3-5: Rep Rows 1 and 2 once, then rep Row 1 once more. BO all sts loosely in rib.

Shoulder Placket (back)**:** Pick up 23(27-27) sts along sleeve edge opening. Beginning at neck edge, work 3 rows in K1, P1 rib in same manner as before. BO all sts.

Shoulder Placket (front)**:** Pick up 23(27-27) sts along front armhole edge beginning at lower edge of placket.

Row 1: Work in K1, P1 rib across, end K1.

Row 2: Buttonhole Row: P1, K1, P1, YO, K2 tog, (K1, P1) 2(3-3) times, K1, YO, K2 tog, (P1, K1) 2(3-3) times, P1, YO, K2 tog, (P1, K1) twice.

Row 3: Work in K1, P1 rib across, end K1. BO all sts. Sew buttons on back placket to correspond with buttonholes. Weave in any yarn ends.

Note: Hat is written in 2 sizes, 6 mos and 12 to 24 mos.

Hat: With larger size needles, CO 96(108) sts loosely.

Cuff: Work in K1, P1 rib for 1".

Turning Ridge:
Purl across.

Patt Row 1: K5(7), ★ P2, (K1, P1, K1, P2) 4 times, K 10(14); rep from ★ once, P2, (K1, P1, K1, P2) 4 times, K 5(7).

Patt Row 2: P5(7), ★ K2, (P3, K2) 4 times, P 10(14); rep from ★ once, K2, (P3, K2) 4 times, P5(7). Rep Patt Rows 1 and 2 until piece measures approx 4½(5)" from CO row, ending by working Patt Row 2.

Crown Shaping
Row 1: K5(7), ★ P2 tog, (K1, P1, K1, P2 tog) 4 times, K 10(14); rep from ★ once, P2 tog, (K1, P1, K1, P2 tog) 4 times, K5(7): 81(93) sts.

Row 2: Purl across.

Row 3: Knit across.

Row 4: Purl across.

Row 5: K2, K2 tog, K1(3), ★ (P1, K1, K2 tog) 4 times, P1, (K2, K2 tog) 2(3) times, K2; rep from ★ once, (P1, K1, K2 tog) 4 times, P1, K1(3), K2 tog, K2: 63(73) sts.

Row 6: Purl across.

Row 7: Knit across.

Row 8: Purl across.

Row 9: ★ K2, K2 tog; rep from ★ across to last 3(1) sts, K3(1).

Row 10: Purl across.

Row 11: Knit across.

Row 12: Purl across.

Row 13: ★ K1, K2 tog; rep from ★ across. Finish off leaving 12" strand; draw yarn thru rem sts, pull up tightly and fasten securely. Turn cuff up along Turning Ridge and sew center back seam.

Ear Flap (make 2)**:** With hat right side facing and cuff turning ridge at top, count 16 sts from back seam on each side of hat; mark 16th st.

(***Note:*** This should be the center of rib Patt on hat.)

Row 1: Pick up and knit 22 sts along turning ridge, ending in center of Stock St Patt.

Row 2: Purl across

Row 3: Knit across.

Row 4: Purl across.

Continue in est patt decreasing one st each edge EOR 7 times: 8 sts.

Next Row: (K2 tog) 4 times. BO rem 4 sts. Attach 9" length of ribbon to each ear flap. See Pompom Instructions on **pg. 3** and make 2" pompom; attach to top of hat.

Note: Booties are written in size 6 mos only.

Bootie (make 2)

With smaller size needles, CO 32 sts. Work Patt Rows 1 and 2. Rep Patt Rows 1 and 2 until piece measures approx $2^1/_2$" from beg, ending by working Patt Row 2; change to larger size needles.

Row 1: K 12, work next 8 sts in est patt, K 12.

Row 2: P 12, work next 8 sts in est patt, P 12.

Row 3 (Eyelet Row)**:** K1, (K2 tog, YO, K1) 3 times, K2 tog, YO, work next 8 sts in est patt, (YO, K2 tog, K1) 4 times.

Row 4: P 12, work next 8 sts in est patt, P 12.

Row 5: K 12, work next 8 sts in est patt, K 12.

Continuing to work on 32 sts, rep Rows 4 and 5 until piece measures approx 1" from Eyelet Row, ending by working Patt Row 2.

Heel Shaping

Row 1: K3, **turn**, slip 1, purl rem 2 sts.

Row 2: K4, **turn**, slip 1, purl rem 3 sts.

Row 3: K5, **turn**, slip 1, purl rem 4 sts.

Row 4: K6, **turn**, slip 1, purl rem 5 sts.

Row 5: K7, **turn**, slip 1, purl rem 6 sts.

Row 6: K 11, P1, work next 8 sts in est patt, P1, K 11.

Row 7: P3, **turn**, slip 1, knit rem 2 sts.

Row 8: P4, **turn**, slip 1, knit rem 3 sts.

Row 9: P5, **turn**, slip 1, knit rem 4 sts.

Row 10: P6, **turn**, slip 1, knit rem 5 sts.

Row 11: P7, **turn**, slip 1, knit rem 6 sts.

Work even in est patt until piece measures approx 6" from beg, ending by working Patt Row 2.

Toe Shaping:

Row 1: K2 tog, K4, K2 tog, K 16, K2 tog, K4, K2 tog: 28 sts.

Row 2: Purl across.

Row 3: K2 tog, K4, K2 tog, K 12, K2 tog, K4, K2 tog: 24 sts.

Row 4: P5, P2 tog, P 10, P2 tog, P5: 22 sts.

Row 5: ★ K1, K2 tog; rep from ★ across, K1. BO rem 15 sts.

Finishing: With right sides tog, sew center back seam and bottom of sole; finish off. Fold piece so that seam is facing and sew across end as indicated by dotted line in **Diagram** to form toe.

Diagram

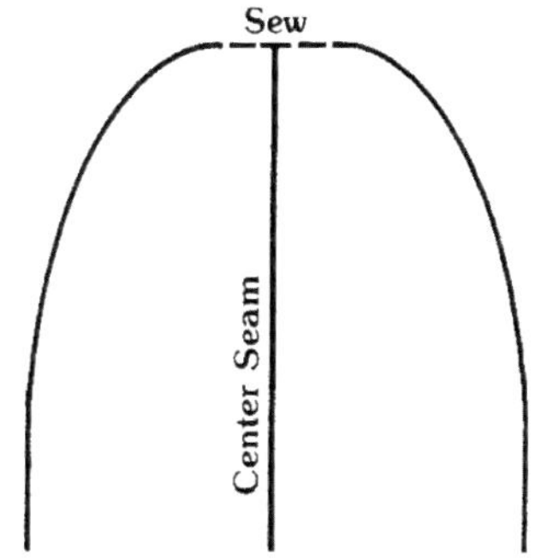

Tie (make 2)**:** With crochet hook, make chain 18" long; weave thru Eyelet Row of bootie beginning on one side of Patt Rows and ending on opposite side of Patt Rows. See Pompom Instructions on **pg. 3** and make 2, (1") pompoms; attach 1 pompom securely to each end of chain.

Knitted
FAIR ISLE SET

BIB OVERALLS & HAT

SIZES:	**6 mos**	**12 mos**	**24 mos**
Approx weight:	to 18 lbs	to 24 lbs	to 30 lbs
Garment Measurements:			
waist	20"	21"	22"
crotch length	$5^1/_2$"	$6^1/_2$"	$7^1/_2$"
leg length	$6^1/_2$"	$7^1/_2$"	$8^1/_2$"

Size Note: Instructions are written in smallest size with changes for larger sizes in parentheses.

MATERIALS: Sport Wt Yarn - white

Set	4(5-6) oz [113.6 (142-170.4) grams]
Overalls	3(4-4.5) oz [85.2 (113.6-127.8) grams]
Hat	1(1-1.5) oz [28.4 (28.4-42.6) grams]

Approx 16(18-22) yds each blue and yellow; straight knitting needles sizes 2 (2.75 mm) and 3 (3.25 mm) or sizes needed for gauge; 2 ($^3/_4$") buttons, 1 yard (1" wide) grosgrain ribbon; **for Tie only**, aluminum crochet hook size E (3.5 mm)

GAUGE: With larger size needles in stock st,
6 sts = 1"; 8 rows = 1"

INSTRUCTIONS

Note: Overalls are worked in two pieces and knitted from the waist down.

Overalls

Right Leg: CO 59(62-65) sts loosely.

Rib Row 1: With smaller size needles and white, ★ K2, P1; rep from ★ across to last 2 sts, K2: 59(62-65) sts.

Rib Row 2: ★ P2, K1; rep from ★ across to last 2 sts, P2: 59(62-65) sts.

Work in est rib for 1", ending by working Rib Row 2. With larger size needles, work next 4 rows in stock st (knit one row, purl one row); mark beg of last row for front edge.

Back Shaping (Short Rows)**:**

Row 1: K 13(15-17), leaving rem sts unworked on left needle, **turn**, slip 1, P 12(14-16).

Row 2: K 18(20-22), **turn**, slip 1, P 17(19-21).

Row 3: K 23(25-27), **turn**, slip 1, P 22(24-26).

Row 4: K 28(30-32), **turn**, slip 1, P 27(29-31).

Row 5: K 33(35-37), **turn**, slip 1, P 32(34-36).

SIZE 12 mos ONLY: Row 6: K 40, **turn**, slip 1, P 39.

SIZE 24 mos ONLY: Row 6: K 42, **turn**, slip 1, P 41.

Row 7: K 47, **turn**, slip 1, P 46.

ALL SIZES: Continuing in stock st and working across 59(62-65) sts, inc one st each side every 6th row, 4(5-6) times: 67(72-77) sts. Work even until piece measures $5^1/_2(6^1/_2-7^1/_2)$", or desired length for crotch.

(*Note:* Measure length of front marked edge).

Crotch and Leg Shaping

BO 3 sts at beg of next 2 rows. Dec one st each side EOR 7(7-6) times: 47(52-59) sts. Work even until Leg measures approx 5(6-7)" from first BO row or 1½" less than desired length, ending by working a knit row.

Next Row: Knit across. (*Note:* Work is now reversed.) When cuff is turned up, reverse stockinette st will be hidden. Continue in reverse stock st (purl one row, knit one row) for 11 more rows, ending by working a purl row.

Inc Row: K 15, inc in next st, K 15, inc in next st, knit across rem sts.

Turning Ridge: Knit across.

Cuff:

Row 1: Knit across.

Row 2: Purl across.

SIZES 6 mos and 24 mos ONLY: Rows 3-9: Working Rows 1-7 of **Chart** in **Fig. 1**, rep A to B, 7(9) times, then A to C once, joining colors as needed.

SIZE 12 mos ONLY: Rows 3-9: Work Rows 1-7 of **Chart** in **Fig. 1**, rep A to B, 9 times joining colors as needed.

ALL SIZES: Row 10: Purl across.

Rows 11-15: Knit each row. BO all sts.

Fig. 1

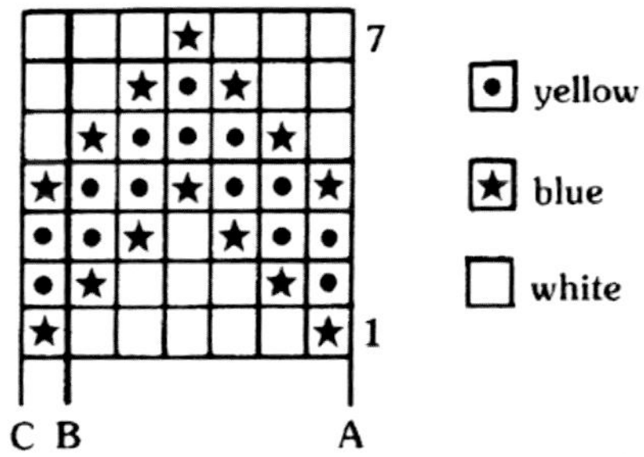

Left Leg: Work ribbing same as right leg. Change to larger size needles. Beginning and ending with knit rows, work next 5 rows in stock st; mark beg of last row for front edge.

Back Shaping (Short Rows)

Row 1: Refer to Right Leg Back Shaping Row 1 and P 13(15-17), **turn**, slip 1, K 12(14-16).

Row 2: P 18(20-22), **turn**, slip 1, K 17(19-21). Continuing in est stock st, work in same manner as Rows 3 thru 5(6-7) of Right Leg Back Shaping. Complete piece same as Right Leg. With pieces right sides tog and white, sew front and back seam. Turn cuff up along Turning Ridge and sew leg seam and cuff tog beginning with one cuff edge and ending with opposite cuff.

Bib

With front facing, count 20 sts to right of center front; with larger size needles and white, pick up 41 sts and knit 6 rows keeping 41 sts in each row.

Patt Row 1 (wrong side)**:** K5, purl across to last 5 sts, K5.

Patt Row 2: Knit across. Rep Bib Patt Rows 1 and 2 until bib measures approx $3^1/_2(4-4^1/_2)$" from beg, ending by working a purl row. Keeping K5 at beg and end of row in est patt, work Rows 1-7 of **Chart** in **Fig. 1** on center 31 sts; rep A to B, 4 times, then A to C once, joining colors as needed.

Next 4 Rows: With white only, Rep Patt Rows 1 and 2 twice.

Garter Stitch Border

Buttonhole Row 1: K6, BO 4 sts, K 21, BO 4 sts, K6.

Buttonhole Row 2: K6, CO 4 sts, K 21, CO 4 sts, K6.

Next 3 Rows: Knit each row. BO all sts.

Right Strap: With back right side facing, count 18(20-22) sts to right of center back seam. With white and larger size needles, pick up 8 sts. working toward center back seam.

Row 1 (wrong side)**:** K2, P4, K2.

Row 2: Knit across. Rep Rows 1 and 2 until strap measures 11" or desired length. BO all sts.

Left Strap: Count 10(12-14) sts to left of center back seam and working away from center back seam, work same as for Right Strap.

Finishing: With matching thread, sew 1" wide grosgrain ribbon full length of each strap turning under 3/8" on each end; sew 3/4" button on end of each strap. Cut 1" wide grosgrain ribbon same length as width of bib plus 3/4". Mark buttonhole placement on ribbon to correspond with buttonholes on bib and make (by machine or by hand) 2 buttonholes. Sew ribbon to wrong side of bib matching buttonholes and turning under 3/8" on each end. Sew bib buttonholes to ribbon buttonholes.

Hat: Cuff: With larger size needles and white, CO 86(92-98) sts loosely. Work in rib same as for Overalls until piece measures approx 1" from beg, ending by working Rib Row 1; dec one st at end of last row: 85(91-97) sts.

Turning Ridge

Knit across.

Next Row: Knit across.

(*Note:* Work is now reversed.)

Work in reverse stock st (purl one row, knit one row) for 4 rows, ending by working a knit row, then knit across next row. Continue in stock st until piece measures 4(4 1/2-4 1/2)", ending by working a purl row. Continuing in stock st, work Rows 1-7 of **Chart** in **Fig. 1, pg. 27**, rep A to B, 13(14-15} times, then A to C once, joining colors as needed.

Next Row: Purl across.

SIZES 6 and 24 mos ONLY: Dec Row: K2 tog, knit across: 84(96) sts.

SIZE 12 mos ONLY: Dec Row: Knit across, decreasing 3 sts evenly spaced: 88 sts.

ALL SIZES: Work in stock st until piece measures approx 5 1/2(6-6)" from beg, ending by working a purl row.

Hat Shaping

Dec Row 1: ★ K2, K2 tog; rep from ★ across: 63(66-72) sts. Work next 3(5-5) rows even in stock st.

Dec Row 2: ★ K1, K2 tog; rep from ★ across: 42(44-48) sts. Work next 3(5-5) rows even in stock st.

Dec Row 3: K2 tog across: 21(22-24) sts. Work next 5(3-3) rows even in stock st. Finish off leaving 12" strand; draw thru all sts, pull up tightly and fasten securely. Turn up cuff along Turning Ridge and sew center back seam. Weave in any yarn ends. See Pompom Instructions on **pg. 3** and make 2" pompom; fasten securely to top of Hat.

***Optional:* Tie** (make 2)**:** Using double strand of yarn and crochet hook, (ch 7, slip st in 2nd ch from hook and in each ch across) twice, slip st in beg ch of first ch-7 (V made); ch 60 or enough to make tie 10" long; finish off. Sew first half of V to hat approx 2" from back seam and second half of V approx 3" from back seam. Rep for second Tie; weave in any yarn ends.

We have made every effort to ensure that these instructions are accurate and complete. We cannot, however, be responsible for human error, typographical mistakes, or variations in individual work.

Cover garments made and patterns tested by Bonnie Coors, Irene Espy, Kate Fitzpatrick, Viginai Hogan, Patti Oonk, Cathy Sahm, Christel Shelton, Nancy Sisk, Mary Kathryn Stein Anne Ullrich, and Annie Mary Wilson.

Made in U.S.A.